FRANCHISING IN MOZAMBIQUE 2014

Legal and Business Considerations

KENDAL H. TYRE, JR., EXECUTIVE EDITOR
DIANA VILMENAY-HAMMOND, MANAGING EDITOR
COURTNEY L. LINDSAY, II, ASSISTANT EDITOR

LEXNOIR FOUNDATION

FOURTH QUARTER 2013

LexNoir Foundation is the charitable, educational arm of LexNoir, an international network of lawyers connecting the African Diaspora.

This publication, *Franchising in Mozambique 2014: Legal and Business Considerations*, contains excerpts from *Franchising in Africa 2014: Legal and Business Considerations*. Both works are published by LexNoir Foundation and reflect the points of view of the authors and editors as of the date of publication and do not necessarily represent the opinions, interpretations, or positions of the law firms or organizations with which they are affiliated, nor the opinions, interpretations or positions of LexNoir Foundation or LexNoir.

Nothing contained in this book is to be considered as the rendering of legal advice, either generally or in connection with any specific issues or case. Readers are responsible for obtaining advice from their own legal counsel or other professional. This book, any forms and agreements or other information herein are intended for educational and informational purposes only.

www.lexnoir.org

Table of Contents

Franchising in Mozambique

Diogo Xavier da Cunha
Miranda Correia Amendoeira & Associados

Bibliography of International Franchise Resources

Kendal H. Tyre, Jr., Diana Vilmenay-Hammond, Pierce Haesung Han, Courtney Lindsay, II and Keri McWilliams
Nixon Peabody LLP

Acknowledgment

This book could not have been written without the hard work and dedication of each of the contributing authors and editors. Thank you.

We would like to acknowledge and extend our heartfelt gratitude to Michael Collier and Maria Stallings of the Washington, D.C. office of Nixon Peabody LLP for their invaluable assistance in revising, proofing, and editing this publication.

About the Editors and Authors

Kendal H. Tyre, Jr. – Kendal is a partner in the Washington, D.C. office of Nixon Peabody LLP. He handles domestic and cross-border transactions, including mergers and acquisitions, joint ventures, strategic alliances, licensing, and franchise matters.

In his franchise and licensing practice, Kendal counsels domestic and international franchisors, franchisees, licensors, licensees and distributors regarding U.S. state and federal franchise laws as well as foreign franchise legislation in a variety of jurisdictions. Kendal drafts and provides advice with regard to franchise and license agreements, disclosure documents and area development agreements and has extensive experience drafting and negotiating a variety of other commercial agreements. His client base spans the United States and foreign countries, including South Africa, Kenya, and the United Kingdom.

Kendal is a frequent contributor to franchise publications and a frequent speaker at franchise programs held by the American Bar Association Forum on Franchising and the International Franchise Association.

Kendal is co-chair of the firm's Diversity Action Committee and its Africa Group. Kendal is also the executive director of LexNoir Foundation.

E-mail address: ktyre@nixonpeabody.com

Diana Vilmenay-Hammond – Diana is an attorney in the Washington, D.C. office of Nixon Peabody LLP. She is a member of the firm's Franchise & Distribution Team.

In her franchise practice, Diana works with domestic and international franchisors on transactional and litigation matters. Specifically, she counsels franchisor clients regarding state and federal franchise laws, disclosure and registration obligations.

Diana drafts and negotiates various commercial agreements, including international franchise and development agreements.

Diana has co-authored numerous articles on franchising and frequently co-hosted the Nixon Peabody franchise law webinar series. Topics have included:

- "Franchise Case Law Round-Up: Implications for Your Franchise," February 15, 2012;
- "Social Media Part II: Best Practices in Protecting Your Brand in the New Media," September 14, 2010; and
- "The Awuah Case: Bellwether or Outlier," May 11, 2010

Diana received her J.D. from Howard University School of Law and her B.A. from Georgetown University. She is a member of the American Bar Association (Forum on Franchising).

Email address: dvilmenay@nixonpeabody.com

Pierce Haesung Han – Pierce is an associate in Nixon Peabody's Global Business & Transactions Group. Pierce focuses his practice on three main areas, assisting clients with a variety of complex business transactions.

- Mergers & Acquisitions: Providing assistance to both public and private clients with various mergers and acquisitions, performing due diligence, drafting and negotiating transaction documents, and facilitating closing and post-closing mechanics.
- International Commercial Transactions: Drafting and negotiating a variety of commercial agreements, including international franchise and development agreements, license agreements, and purchase and sale agreements.
- Federal Securities Law Matters: Assisting public and private clients regarding federal securities laws and stock exchange rules relating to corporate governance and disclosure.

Pierce serves as the Secretary of the Asian Pacific Bar Association Educational Fund (an affiliate of the Asian Pacific American Bar Association of the Greater Washington, D.C. Area).

Pierce received his J.D. from Georgetown University Law Center and his B.A. from Case Western Reserve University. He is admitted to practice in the State of New York and the District of Columbia.

E-mail address: phan@nixonpeabody.com

Courtney L. Lindsay II – Courtney is an associate in Nixon Peabody's Corporate and Finance practice. In his corporate practice, Courtney assists for-profit and non-profit entities with transactional matters and corporate governance. In various capacities, Courtney has been involved in multiple merger and acquisition transactions, including drafting and managing due diligence.

Previously, Courtney worked in the legal and business affairs department at a national cable network, where he handled matters related to the network's LLC agreement, including drafting board and member consent agreements.

Courtney received his J.D. from the University of Virginia School of Law and his B.A. from the University of Virginia. He is admitted to practice in the Commonwealth of Virginia and the District of Columbia.

E-mail address: clindsay@nixonpeabody.com

Keri McWilliams – Keri is an associate in the Franchise & Distribution team of Nixon Peabody LLP. Keri works with clients on a number of franchising issues, including obtaining and maintaining franchise registrations in various states, responding to state inquiries regarding trade practices, ongoing compliance with state and federal regulations, and updating franchise disclosure documents. She also handles franchise sales counseling and franchise system issues.

Keri is a member of the American Bar Association's Forum on Franchising, and the Federal and Minnesota State bar associations. She is also a member of Minnesota Women Lawyers and the Minnesota Association of Black Lawyers, and a volunteer in the Volunteer Lawyers Network.

Keri received her J.D. from the Georgetown University Law Center and her B.F.A. from Washington University. She is admitted to practice in the District of Columbia and Minnesota.

E-mail address: kmcwilliams@nixonpeabody.com

Diogo Xavier Da Cunha – Diogo is the partner responsible for the Mozambique-related practice of Lisbon-based international law firm Miranda Correia Amendoeira & Associados. He currently provides legal advice to a number of international companies doing business in Portugal and Mozambique.

Diogo's practice is predominantly of a corporate/commercial nature, with a strong energy and distribution component. He is regularly involved in a wide range of corporate transactions and has advised oil, mining, energy and other international and Portuguese companies in respect of various legal issues, such as company acquisitions, international commercial arbitration, oil & gas agreements, energy law, contract and company law and, in general, foreign investment operations.

Diogo is a regular contributor to several newspapers and legal bulletins, and has published articles and studies on several fields of law. He was ranked as an Expert in Corporate and M&A in the 2007 to 2013 editions of the European Legal Experts Guide. He is fluent in English, Spanish and French.

E-mail address: Diogo.Cunha@mirandalawfirm.com

About the Book

Franchising in Mozambique 2014: Legal and Business Considerations contains excerpts from the larger work, *Franchising in Africa 2014: Legal and Business Considerations.* Both books serve as practical, succinct, easy-to-use reference tools for lawyers, business people and academics to use in navigating the myriad laws and business issues impacting franchise arrangements on the African continent.

This book provides an overview of the franchise industry in Mozambique and addresses the typical legal issues confronted when expanding a franchise system in Mozambique. The larger work, *Franchising in Africa 2014: Legal and Business Considerations*, covers those laws governing franchising in fifteen other African countries – Angola, Botswana, Burundi, Cape Verde, Democratic Republic of Congo, Egypt, Ethiopia, Ghana, Kenya, Nigeria, Rwanda, South Africa, Tunisia, Zambia and Zimbabwe.

In both books, an author, who is a legal expert in the designated jurisdiction, addresses the basic questions that a franchise lawyer would need to know to competently represent a client in expanding their franchise system to that country.

Each country chapter organizes a discussion of that country's laws under various headings and in a uniform format. Topics were sent to each country's author in the form of a questionnaire, and each author drafted responses to the questions presented. A general overview relating to the political and economic history of the country at the beginning of each chapter provides an initial context for the regulatory framework. [1]

---

[1] The source of information for these sections is the Central Intelligence Agency, https://www.cia.gov/library/publications/the-world-factbook/ (last visited November 3, 2013).

Apart from an overview of the legal framework for franchising, each book contains other articles and resources that should prove useful to those in the franchise industry.

The authors for each chapter are listed at the beginning of a chapter and their biographical information is listed in the previous section, *About the Editors and Authors*.

Readers should always consult with local counsel in the relevant jurisdiction instead of relying solely on the information contained in this book. The laws governing franchising are evolving and local counsel in Mozambique are best positioned to provide timely, relevant advice applying the current law to the particular facts of a case.

Franchising in Mozambique

Diogo Xavier da Cunha

Miranda Correia Amendoeira & Associados

Lisbon, Portugal

Mozambique

I. Introduction

A. Historical Background of Country

Almost five centuries as a Portuguese colony came to a close for Mozambique when it became independent in 1975. Large-scale emigration, economic dependence on South Africa, a severe drought, and a prolonged civil war hindered the country's development until the mid-1990s. The ruling party, the Front for the Liberation of Mozambique (FRELIMO) formally abandoned Marxism in 1989, and the new constitution provided for multiparty elections and a free market economy. In 1992, a United Nations negotiated peace agreement between FRELIMO and rebel Mozambique National Resistance forces ended the civil war. In December 2004, Mozambique underwent a delicate transition when Joaquim Chissano stepped down after being in office for 18 years. His successor Armando Emilio Guebuza, promised to continue the sound economic policies that have encouraged foreign investment.

B. Economy of the Country

Soon after its independence in 1975, Mozambique was one of the world's poorest countries. The mismanagement of the country and a brutal civil war (1977-1992) worsened the situation. In 1987, the government embraced a series of macroeconomic reforms designed to stabilize the economy. These reforms, combined with monetary assistance and political stability (since the multi-party elections in 1994) have drastically improved the country's growth rate. Monetary reforms have reduced inflation. Fiscal reforms, the introduction of a value-added tax, and the reform of the customs service, have improved the revenue collection abilities of the government. A substantial trade imbalance persists, although the opening of the Mozal aluminum smelter (the country's largest foreign investment project to date) has increased export earnings.

At the end of 2007, and after years of negotiations, the government took over Portugal's majority share of the Cahora

Bassa Hydroelectricity Company (CBHC). CBHC was a dam, which was not transferred to Mozambique after independence because of the ensuing civil war and its unpaid debts. More energy power is needed for additional investment projects in titanium extraction, processing, and garment manufacturing. These projects could further close the import/export gap. Mozambique's substantial foreign debt has been reduced through forgiveness and rescheduling under the IMF's Heavily Indebted Poor Countries (HIPC) and Enhanced HIPC initiatives, and it is now at a manageable level.

In July 2007, the Millennium Challenge Corporation signed a Compact with Mozambique. The Compact entered into force in September 2008 and will continue for five years. Compact projects will continue to focus on improving sanitation, roads, agriculture, and the business regulation environment in an effort to spur economic growth in the four northern provinces of the country. Mozambique grew at an average annual rate of 9% for most of the past decade. It is one of Africa's strongest performances. However, heavy reliance on aluminum, which accounts for about one-third of exports, subjects the economy to volatile international prices. The sharp decline in aluminum prices during the global economic crisis lowered the GDP growth by several percentage points.

In an attempt to mantain the cost of living low, the government implemented subsidies, decreased taxes and tariffs, and instituted other fiscal measures. Real growth of 7.2% was achieved in 2011.

C. Franchise Legal Overview

Despite some scattered provisions, there is no specific legal regime for franchising under Mozambican law.

In the absence of a specific regime, a franchise agreement is seen as an agreement between two parties in the exercise of a commercial activity, albeit an atypical commercial agreement. See the legal regime for which is set forth in the Mozambican

Commercial Code (approved by *Decree-law No. 2/2005, of December 27, 2005, as amended*) ("Commercial Code").

The contractual relationship (i.e., the rights and obligations) established between the parties in a franchise agreement is construed in accordance with the provisions of the Mozambican Civil Code (approved by *Decree-law No. 47344, of November 25, 1966, as amended*) ("Civil Code").

II. Regulatory Requirements

A. Pre-Sale Disclosure

Please describe any pre-sale franchise disclosure or similar requirements that may apply to franchise transactions.

No pre-sale disclosure or similar requirements apply to franchise transactions under the laws of Mozambique.

B. Governmental Approvals, Registrations, Filing Requirements

Please describe any necessary government approvals, registrations, or filing requirements that may apply to franchise transactions.

Other than the registration requirements referred to below - see Section III (Currency) and Section V (Trademarks) -, no government approval, registration, or filing requirements apply specifically to franchise transactions.

C. Limits of Fees and Typical Term of Franchise Agreement

Please describe any limits upon the nature and extent of fees and the term of a typical franchise agreement.

As mentioned in Section I, since there is no specific regime governing the franchise agreement, parties are free to agree on the terms and conditions of a franchise agreement, subject to certain limits imposed by the Commercial Code and/or the Civil Code. The agreement must also always be in compliance with public policy principles of Mozambican law. Other than those caveats, there are no limits upon the nature and extent of fees or the term of a typical franchise agreement.

III. Currency

If all payments under a franchise agreement must be made in immediately available U.S. Dollars, please advise as to any restrictions, reporting requirements, or regulations concerning the exchange, repatriation, or remittance of U.S. Dollars.

According to Mozambican law, payments under a franchise agreement do not need to be made in immediately available U.S. Dollars.

Foreign exchange rules currently applicable in Mozambique are contained in (i) the *Foreign Exchange Law*, approved by *Law 11/2009, of March 11, 2009*; (ii) the *Foreign Exchange Regulations*, approved by *Decree 83/2010, of 13 December, 2010*; and (iii) other ancillary regulations, including a number of instructions and orders of BoM, such as *BoM Order 6/GGBM/2005, of May 25, 2005, as amended*, which approved rules applicable to the import and export of goods and services.

BoM acts as the foreign exchange control authority and plays a decisive role in terms of the repatriation or payment of funds outside Mozambique. Any such transactions are subject to a prior authorization issued by BoM on a case-by-case basis. Essentially, under the current laws and regulations, any currency transfers between resident and non-resident entities are subject to different requirements depending on the nature of the underlying transaction.

Inflows of currency are subject to registration with BoM. Outflows (such as payments of the royalties and franchise fees to the franchisor) are subject to BoM's approval. The franchise agreement under which payments are being made is also subject to approval by the Ministry of Finance.

Payments made by Mozambican entities (i.e., the franchisee) to Mozambican bank accounts or other Mozambique resident entities (i.e., the franchisor) are free and not subject to any foreign exchange control.

IV. Taxes, Tariffs, and Duties

Please do not provide any in-depth comments on tax structuring. However, please provide your general comments on the typical amount of withholding tax that would apply and whether a "gross-up" provision contained in a franchise agreement would be enforceable in your country.

The Mozambican tax framework adopts a unitary income-tax system.

A. Applicable Rate

Services or fee payments (such as the payments made under a franchise agreement) made by resident entities to non-resident entities are subject to a 20% corporate income tax. This tax liability can be minimized if the entity receiving the payments is incorporated in a country with which Mozambique has a double taxation agreement. At the moment, South Africa, Portugal, Italy, the United Arab Emirates, Mauritius, Macau, India, Vietnam and Botswana are the only countries that have a double taxation agreement with Mozambique.

B. Gross-up Clauses

Gross-up provisions are permitted—and even common—under Mozambican contractual practice and franchise agreements are not an exception.

V. Trademarks

Please advise us as to whether there are any special requirements for granting a valid trademark license, including the use of a registered user agreement or a short trademark license agreement and any required filing of such an agreement with the trademark authorities.

Intellectual property in Mozambique is regulated by the *Mozambican Industrial Property Code* (*Código de Propriedade Industrial de Mozambique*), which was approved by the *Council of Ministers' Decree 4/2006 of April 12, 2006*. Article 122 of that Code is the specific provision governing licensing agreements for trademarks. It establishes a very liberalized l for entering into and enforcing licensing agreements. Under paragraph (1) of Article 122, owners of a trademark are entitled to enter into contracts to license use of that trademark to others. This same paragraph is unambiguous in its subsequent statement that such licensing will not deprive the owner of its rights of effective control over its products or services' specifications, their nature or quality.

Under paragraph (2) of the Article, which deals with the enforceability of such agreements, the owner of the trademark may also grant the licensee powers to defend the trademark against breaches without depriving itself of any of its own rights in that respect.

Moreover, the enforcement of the licensing agreement vis-à-vis third parties is subject to notification of the agreement to the trademark office (*IPI—Instituto da Propriedade Industrial*), as specified in paragraph (3) of Article 122.

VI. Restrictions on Transfer

Please advise as to whether there are any restrictions (1) on a franchisor to restrict transfers by a master franchisee, any interest in a master franchisee, or the assets of the master franchisee or (2) the ability of a master franchisee to control and/or restrict transfers of a subfranchisee's rights under a master franchise agreement, interest in the subfranchisee, or the assets of the subfranchisee.

A. In Relation to Master Franchisee

As referred to in Section I.C., under Mozambican law there is no specific legal regime to govern the franchise agreement. The parties may agree to adopt any provision, which is not against the law. The restrictions on transfer referred to above do not violate the law, and as such, may be included in a franchise agreement.

1. Assignment.

According to the Civil Code, neither party may assign its contractual position without the prior consent of the other party. While it is common for franchise agreements to condition the franchisee's right to assign its contractual position with the consent of the franchisor, it also applies automatically per direct operation of the law in case the agreement does not expressly provide for such a rule.

2. Change of Control.

It is permissible, under Mozambican law, to subject to the consent of the franchisor the right of the franchisee's shareholders (and the respective group members) to transfer their (direct and/or indirect) interests in the share capital of the franchisee.

3. Transfer of Assets.

A clause by virtue of which the franchisee becomes obliged upon termination of the franchise agreement to transfer to the franchisor (or to another entity designated by the franchisor) all the assets used in the franchise is permissible and common in franchise agreements. The parties are free to determine whether such provision shall be included in the agreement, and if so, the mechanism to calculate the value of these assets.

B. In Relation to Subfranchisees.

1. Assignment.

As referred to in Section VI.A.1., according to the Civil Code, neither the master franchisee nor the subfranchisee may assign its contractual position without the prior consent of the other. Therefore, although not expressly provided for in the subfranchise agreement, a party may not assign its contractual position without the other's approval.

Moreover, the parties may also agree to subject the subfranchisee's right to assign its contractual position to the consent of the franchisor.

2. Change of Control.

As previously mentioned in Section VI.A.2., it is possible, under Mozambican law, to subject to the consent of the master franchisee the right of the subfranchisee's shareholders (and the respective group members) to transfer their interests in the share capital of the subfranchisee.

Also, the parties may further agree that the subfranchisee's shareholders (and their group companies) may only transfer their (direct and/or indirect) interests in the subfranchisee's share capital upon the master franchisee's approval.

3. Transfer of Assets.

As mentioned in Section VI.A.3., a clause by virtue of which the subfranchisee becomes obliged, upon termination of the subfranchise agreement, to transfer to the master franchisee (or to another entity designated by the master franchisee) all the assets used in the subfranchise agreement is permissible and also common in these types of agreements.

A provision may also be included in the agreement to obligate the subfranchisee to transfer to the franchisor the relevant assets upon termination of the subfranchise agreement.

It is entirely up to the parties whether such provisions are included in the agreement, and if so, the mechanism that is to be used to calculate the value of these assets.

VII. Termination

Please advise us as to any laws relating to termination in your country, such as agency laws, required indemnity provisions, notice or "good cause" requirements, or other laws affecting termination of a franchise agreement. Please describe.

As mentioned above in Section I.C., in the absence of a specific regime governing the franchise agreement, causes for termination of the agreement are those that are commonly accepted by law, such as (i) mutual agreement, (ii) unilateral termination, and (iii) the occurrence or nonoccurrence of any of the events agreed upon by the parties to constitute a cause for termination.

VIII. Governing Law, Jurisdiction, and Dispute Resolution

A. Choice of Law of Foreign Jurisdiction

Please confirm whether the choice of law of a foreign jurisdiction would likely to be upheld under the law of the country, except for certain matters such as trademarks, bankruptcy, and competition matters, which we assume would be governed by the law in your country.

Under the Civil Code, the parties may freely declare their transactions to be subject to a particular jurisdiction of their choice, including foreign jurisdictions. The party's choice of law, however, is not totally free. It must reflect a serious interest by the parties in having some connection with either any of the elements of the agreement, or some connection with the chosen foreign jurisdiction.

Moreover, it is worth noting that under conflict of laws' principles, a choice of foreign law will not be permissible when it violates fundamental principles of Mozambican public policy, and the chosen law does not provide an alternative solution consistent with those principles. This means that the Mozambican court would apply the foreign law, but where the solution given by the foreign law is deemed to be offensive to Mozambique's public policy rules, the court would apply Mozambican law to the extent necessary to avoid such offence.

Also, where such agreements might be subject to any licenses or registration formalities (e.g., registration of trademark licensing agreements), the enforceability of the agreements shall be dependent on the compliance with any applicable formalities (see Section III).

B. International Arbitration Dispute Resolution

Please confirm that a court in your country would honor an election of international arbitration dispute resolution, and therefore refuse to hear any disputes arising under a franchise agreement.

The Mozambican legal framework governing arbitration is set forth in the *Arbitration, Conciliation and Mediation Law—Law 11/99, of July 8, 1999* (the "ACML"). The ACML is a fairly modern and sophisticated statute, which is primarily based on the Portuguese Arbitration Law.

The definition of international arbitration set out in the ACML follows the one adopted in the *1985 Model Law on International Commercial Arbitration of the United Nations Commission on International Trade Law* ("UNCITRAL"). International arbitration is defined as an arbitration in which international trade interests are at stake. The ACML then lists several instances where it deems that international trade interests are at stake. It includes circumstances where the parties to the arbitration are residents of different countries.

Under ACML, the parties are free to choose international arbitration rules (whether institutional or ad hoc rules) to govern the arbitration. Generally, the parties may choose a foreign country as the seat for arbitration proceedings.

Mozambican courts will uphold the judgment of a foreign court or a foreign arbitration award. However, the judgment would first have to undergo a review and confirmation process in the Mozambican courts. The procedure to have a foreign arbitral award recognized and enforced through the Mozambican courts is made in accordance with the *Convention on the Recognition and Enforcement of Foreign Arbitral Awards* (the "New York Convention") – to which Mozambique is a party.

The local courts' ability to challenge, to intervene, or accept an appeal from an arbitration/arbitral award varies depending on whether it is a (i) local arbitration/arbitral award or (ii) an international arbitration/arbitral award.

Local courts cannot challenge or intervene in a local arbitration / arbitral award. They may, however, accept an appeal for the annulment of the arbitral award in the following situations:

- one of the parties was under some incapacity;
- the agreement is not valid under the law to which the parties have subjected it or, if there is no such law indicated, under Mozambican law;
- a party against whom the award is invoked was not given proper notice of the appointment of the arbitrator or of the arbitration proceedings or was otherwise unable to present its case;
- the award does not fall within the terms of the submission to arbitration, or it contains decisions on matters beyond the

scope of the submission to arbitration, though the decisions on matters submitted to arbitration can be separated from those not so submitted, in which case only the latter category will be subject to annulment;

- the composition of the arbitral authority or the arbitral procedure was not in accordance with the agreement of the parties, or, was not in accordance with Mozambican law;

- the subject matter of the disagreement between the parties is not capable of settlement by arbitration under Mozambican law; or

- the recognition or enforcement of the award would be contrary to Mozambican public policy.

Local courts cannot challenge, intervene, or accept any appeal from international arbitration/arbitral awards. Moreover, as noted above, Mozambique is a party to the New York Convention, whereby the recognition and enforcement of the award may only be refused by the local courts in the situations listed in the convention and which are very similar to those described in subsections (a) – (g) above. However, as Mozambican courts are still fairly inexperienced when it comes to enforcement of foreign arbitral awards pursuant to the New York Convention, it is quite likely that unexpected problems will arise when one simply seeks to apply the terms and conditions set forth therein. Accordingly, obtaining recognition of a foreign arbitral award from the Mozambican courts may not be a straightforward exercise.

IX. Non-Competition Provisions

If the franchise agreement prohibits the master franchisee from engaging in certain competitive activities during the term of the agreement, and for a 12-month period after the termination or expiration of the agreement, please comment on the enforceability of non-competition covenants in your country.

Under Mozambican Commercial Code, the parties in a franchise agreement may freely agree on non-competition provisions, such as a prohibition on the franchisee of engaging in certain competitive activities during the term of the agreement and for a 12-month period after the termination or expiration of the agreement. Such provisions would be considered enforceable.

It is common to extend the prohibition of competition (i) to affiliates and related persons/entities of the franchisee and (ii) for a certain period after termination of the franchise agreement. However, as previously referenced in Section I.C., as a non-regulated agreement, the parties to a franchise agreement are free to agree on a non-competition provision, so long as its terms are always in compliance with general public policy principles of Mozambican law and are not deemed inconsistent with the anti-trust rules approved by Law 10/20/13, of April 11, 2013.

X. Language Requirements

Does the law in your country require that a franchise agreement be translated into the local language in order to be enforceable between the parties?

According to Article 459 of the Commercial Code, commercial agreements are valid irrespective of their language. However, if an agreement is to be filed with any public authority in a foreign language, a sworn translation in Portuguese shall be required.

XI. Other Significant Matters

Please advise as to whether there are any significant matters not addressed above of which a franchisor should be aware in connection with its entering into a franchise agreement in your country.

There are no other significant matters to be addressed

Mozambique

Bibliography of International Franchise Resources

Kendal H. Tyre, Jr., Diana Vilmenay-Hammond, Pierce Haesung Han, Courtney Lindsay, II and Keri McWilliams

Nixon Peabody LLP

Washington, D.C.

I. General International Resources

Mark Abell, Gary R. Duvall, and Andrea Oricchio Kirsh, *International Franchise Legislation* B1, ABA FORUM ON FRANCHISING (1996)

Kathleen C. Anderson and Anthony M. Stiegler, *Put Muscle in Your Marks: Enforcing Intellectual Property Rights* W14, ABA FORUM ON FRANCHISING (1995)

Richard M. Asbill and Jane W. LaFranchi, *International Franchise Sales Laws—A Survey* W7, ABA FORUM ON FRANCHISING (2005)

Jeffery A. Brimer, Alison C. McElroy, and John Pratt, *Going International: What Additional Restraints Will You Face?* W4, ABA FORUM ON FRANCHISING (2011)

Michael G. Brennan, Alexander Konigsberg, and Philip F. Zeidman, *Globetrotting: A Workshop on International Franchising* 10/W8, ABA FORUM ON FRANCHISING (1994)

Michael G. Brennan, Alexander Konigsberg, and Philip F. Zeidman, *Globetrotting: Strategies for Launching U.S. Franchisors Abroad* 2/P2, ABA FORUM ON FRANCHISING (1994)

Christopher P. Bussert and Jennifer Dolman, *Regaining Your Trademark After Abandonment or Misappropriation* W7, ABA FORUM ON FRANCHISING (2011)

Ronald T. Coleman and Linda K. Stevens, *Trade Secrets and Confidential Information: Rights and Remedies* W2, ABA FORUM ON FRANCHISING (2000)

Finola Cunningham, *Commerce Department Helps Franchisors Go Global*, in FRANCHISING WORLD 63 (Dec. 2005)

Michael R. Daigle and Alex S. Konigsberg, *Meeting Off-Shore Disclosure and Contract Requirements* F/W13, ABA FORUM ON FRANCHISING (1992)

Jennifer Dolman, Robert A. Lauer, and Lawrence M. Weinberg, *Structuring International Master Franchise Relationships for Success and Responding When Things Go Awry* W22, ABA FORUM ON FRANCHISING (2007)

Gary R. Duvall, Paul Jones, and Jane LaFranchi, *Planning for the International Enforcement of Franchise Agreements* W6, ABA FORUM ON FRANCHISING (1999)

William Edwards, *International Expansion: Do Opportunities Outweigh Challenges?* in FRANCHISING WORLD (February 2008)

George J. Eydt and Stuart Hershman, *Bringing a Foreign Franchise System to the United States* W9, ABA FORUM ON FRANCHISING (2009)

William A. Finkelstein and Louis T. Pirkey, *International Trademarks* W15, ABA FORUM ON FRANCHISING (1991)

William A. Finkelstein, *Protecting Trademarks Internationally: Current Strategies and Developments* B3, ABA FORUM ON FRANCHISING (1996)

Stephen Giles, Lou H. Jones, and Lawrence Weinberg, *Negotiating and Documenting Complex International Franchise Agreements* W21, ABA FORUM ON FRANCHISING (2006)

Steven M. Goldman, Stephen Giles, Marc Israel, and Stanley Wong, *Competition Round Up from Around the World* LB2, ABA FORUM ON FRANCHISING (2004)

David C. Gryce and E. Lynn Perry, *Trademarks and Copyrights in the International Arena* 6/W4, ABA FORUM ON FRANCHISING (1993)

Kenneth S. Kaplan, Andrew P. Loewinger, and Penelope J. Ward, *System Standards in International Franchising* W14, ABA FORUM ON FRANCHISING (2005)

Edward Levitt and Jorge Mondragon, *A Survey of International Legal Traps and How to Avoid Them—Beyond the Franchise Laws* W20, ABA FORUM ON FRANCHISING (2007)

Ned Levitt, Kendal H. Tyre, and Penny Ward, *The Impossible Dream: Controlling Your International Franchise System* W4, ABA FORUM ON FRANCHISING (2010)

Michael K. Lindsey and Andrew P. Loewinger, *International (Non-U.S.) Franchise Disclosure Requirements* W9, ABA FORUM ON FRANCHISING (2002)

Andrew P. Loewinger and John Pratt, *Recent Changes and Trends in International Franchise Laws* W4, ABA FORUM ON FRANCHISING (2008)

Andrew P. Loewinger and Thomas M. Pitegoff, *Avoiding the Long Arm of the Law in International Franchising: Issues and Approaches* W8, ABA FORUM ON FRANCHISING (1995)

Craig J. Madson and Katherine C. Spelman, *Similarity and Confusion in the Intellectual Property Arena* W11, ABA FORUM ON FRANCHISING (1997)

Christopher A. Nowak, John Pratt, and Carl E. Zwisler, *Franchising Internationally with Countries with Opaque Legal Systems* W20, ABA FORUM ON FRANCHISING (2006)

E. Lynn Perry and John L. Sullivan Jr., *Trademark Compliance and Enforcement Techniques* E/W12, ABA FORUM ON FRANCHISING (1992)

Marcel Portmann, *Franchising Sector Proves Global Reach*, in FRANCHISING WORLD (January 2007)

John Pratt and Luiz Henrique O. do Amaral, *Civil Law for Common Law Practitioners (or How to Draft an Agreement for Use Overseas)* W4, ABA FORUM ON FRANCHISING (2002)

Kirk W. Reilly, Robert F. Salkowski and Geoffrey B. Shaw, *Determining the Rules of Engagement in Litigation Here and Abroad* W5, ABA FORUM ON FRANCHISING (2008)

Catherine Riesterer and Frank Zaid, *Basics of International Franchising* L/B2, ABA FORUM ON FRANCHISING (1997)

W. Andrew Scott and Christopher N. Wormald, *Stranger in a Strange Land: Contrasting Franchising in International Expansion* W2, ABA FORUM ON FRANCHISING (2003)

Donald Smith and Erik Wulff, *International Franchising: The Unraveling of an International Franchise Relationship* 15/W13, ABA FORUM ON FRANCHISING (1993)

Frank Zaid, Pamela Mills, and Michael Santa Maria, *Essential Issues in International Franchising* LB/1, ABA FORUM ON FRANCHISING (2001)

II. African Resources

Joyce G. Mazero and J. Perry Maisonneuve, *Franchising in the Middle East and North Africa* W2, ABA FORUM ON FRANCHISING (2009)

Kendal H. Tyre, Jr. and Diana Vilmenay-Hammond, *Franchise World: A Burgeoning Middle Class Spurs Franchise Investment in Africa*, MINORITY BUSINESS ENTREPRENEUR (November 2012)

Kendal H. Tyre, Jr., *IP Protection May Promote Additional Franchise Growth in Africa*, NIXON PEABODY LLP: FRANCHISING BUSINESS & LAW ALERT (September 2012)

Kendal H. Tyre, Jr., *Market Potential for Franchising in Africa*, NIXON PEABODY LLP: FRANCHISING BUSINESS & LAW ALERT (June 2011)

Kendal H. Tyre, Jr. and Courtney L. Lindsay, II, *Continued Growth of Franchising in Africa*, NIXON PEABODY LLP: FRANCHISE LAW ALERT (April 2013)

Kendal H. Tyre, Jr. and Courtney L. Lindsay, II, *Pan African Franchise Federation Holds Inaugural Meeting*, NIXON PEABODY LLP: AFRICA ALERT (June 2013)

Kendal H. Tyre, Jr. and Courtney L. Lindsay, II, *White House Encouraging Private Investment and Transparency in Sub-Saharan Africa*, NIXON PEABODY LLP: AFRICA ALERT (August 2012)

Kendal H. Tyre, Jr. and Diana Vilmenay-Hammond, *African Economic Growth Impacts Franchising on the Continent*, NIXON PEABODY LLP: FRANCHISE LAW ALERT (July 2012)

Kendal H. Tyre, Jr. and Diana Vilmenay-Hammond, *Franchising in Africa*, in FRANCHISING WORLD (August 2013)

John Sotos and Sam Hall, *African Franchising: Cross-Continent Momentum*, in FRANCHISING WORLD (June 2007)

A. Angola

João Afonso Fialho, *Franchising in Angola*, in FRANCHISING IN AFRICA: LEGAL AND BUSINESS CONSIDERATIONS 91-105 (Kendal H. Tyre, Jr. & Diana Vilmenay-Hammond eds. 2012)

B. Botswana

Bonzo Makgalemele, *Franchising in Botswana*, in FRANCHISING IN AFRICA: LEGAL AND BUSINESS CONSIDERATIONS 107-117 (Kendal H. Tyre, Jr. & Diana Vilmenay-Hammond eds. 2012)

C. Cape Verde

João Afonso Fialho, *Franchising in Cape Verde*, in FRANCHISING IN AFRICA: LEGAL AND BUSINESS CONSIDERATIONS 119-132 (Kendal H. Tyre, Jr. & Diana Vilmenay-Hammond eds. 2012)

D. Egypt

Girgis Abd El-Shahid, *Franchising in Eqypt*, in FRANCHISING IN AFRICA: LEGAL AND BUSINESS CONSIDERATIONS 133-142 (Kendal H. Tyre, Jr. & Diana Vilmenay-Hammond eds. 2012)

A. Safaa El Din El Oteifi, *Egypt*, in INTERNATIONAL FRANCHISING EGY/1 (Dennis Campbell gen. ed. 2011)

E. Ethiopia

Yohannes Assefa and Biset Beyene Molla, *Franchising in Ethiopia*, in FRANCHISING IN AFRICA: LEGAL AND BUSINESS CONSIDERATIONS 143-157 (Kendal H. Tyre, Jr. & Diana Vilmenay-Hammond eds. 2012)

Kendal H. Tyre, Jr., Yohannes Assefa and Getachew Mengistie Alemu, *New Intellectual Property Regulation Requires Scramble to Protect Marks in Ethiopia*, NIXON PEABODY LLP: AFRICA ALERT (October 2013)

F. Ghana

Divine K.D. Letsa and Hawa Tejansie Ajei, *Franchising in Ghana*, in FRANCHISING IN AFRICA: LEGAL AND BUSINESS CONSIDERATIONS 159-167 (Kendal H. Tyre, Jr. & Diana Vilmenay-Hammond eds. 2012)

G. Libya

Kendal H. Tyre, Jr. & Diana Vilmenay-Hammond, *First U.S. Franchise Opens in Libya*, NIXON PEABODY LLP: AFRICA ALERT (August 2012)

H. Mozambique

Diogo Xavier da Cunha, *Franchising in Mozambique*, in FRANCHISING IN AFRICA: LEGAL AND BUSINESS CONSIDERATIONS 169-182 (Kendal H. Tyre, Jr. & Diana Vilmenay-Hammond eds. 2012)

I. Nigeria

Theo Emuwa and Bimbola Fowler-Ekar, *Franchising in Nigeria*, in FRANCHISING IN AFRICA: LEGAL AND BUSINESS CONSIDERATIONS 183-198 (Kendal H. Tyre, Jr. & Diana Vilmenay-Hammond eds. 2012)

Kendal H. Tyre, Jr. and Theo Emuwa, *Nigerian Franchising: Making Your Way Through the Thicket*, NIXON PEABODY LLP: FRANCHISE LAW ALERT (June 2005)

J. South Africa

Eugene Honey, *Franchising and the New Consumer Protection Bill*, BOWMAN GILFILLAN (March 2008)

Eugene Honey, *Franchising and the Consumer Protection Bill*, BOWMAN GILFILLAN (May 2008)

Eugene Honey, *Pitfalls and Difficulties with the CPA*, ADAMS & ADAMS (March 2013)

Eugene Honey, *Disclosure is Compulsory*, ADAMS & ADAMS (May 2013)

Eugene Honey and Wim Alberts, *Fundamental Consumer Rights: The Right to Equality*, BOWMAN GILFILLAN (March 2009)

Eugene Honey and Wim Alberts, *The Reach of the Consumer Protection Bill: The Final*, BOWMAN GILFILLAN (March 2009)

Eugene Honey, *South Africa*, in GETTING THE DEAL THROUGH: FRANCHISE (2013) 172-178 (Philip F. Zeidman ed. 2013)

Taswell Papier, *Franchising in South Africa*, in FRANCHISING IN AFRICA: LEGAL AND BUSINESS CONSIDERATIONS 199-224 (Kendal H. Tyre, Jr. & Diana Vilmenay-Hammond eds. 2012)

Kendal H. Tyre, Jr., *A New Legal Landscape for Franchising in South Africa*, NIXON PEABODY LLP: FRANCHISING BUSINESS & LAW ALERT (September 2009)

K. Tunisia

Yessine Ferah, *Franchising in Tunisia*, in FRANCHISING IN AFRICA: LEGAL AND BUSINESS CONSIDERATIONS 225-245 (Kendal H. Tyre, Jr. & Diana Vilmenay-Hammond eds. 2012)

Kendal H. Tyre, Jr., Diana Vilmenay-Hammond, and Yessine Ferah, *New Franchise Legislation in Tunisia*, NIXON PEABODY LLP: FRANCHISE LAW ALERT (September 2010)

L. Zambia

Mabvuto Sakala, *Franchising in Zambia*, in FRANCHISING IN AFRICA: LEGAL AND BUSINESS CONSIDERATIONS 247-255 (Kendal H. Tyre, Jr. & Diana Vilmenay-Hammond eds. 2012)

14722567.1

Printed in Dunstable, United Kingdom

91343675R00030